Animals of...
Scotland

Sloth Dreams Publishing LLC
Published by Sloth Dreams Publishing
Sloth Dreams Children's Books
Pennsylvania, USA

http://www.SlothDreams.com/kids

ISBN: 978-3-9485-6225-0

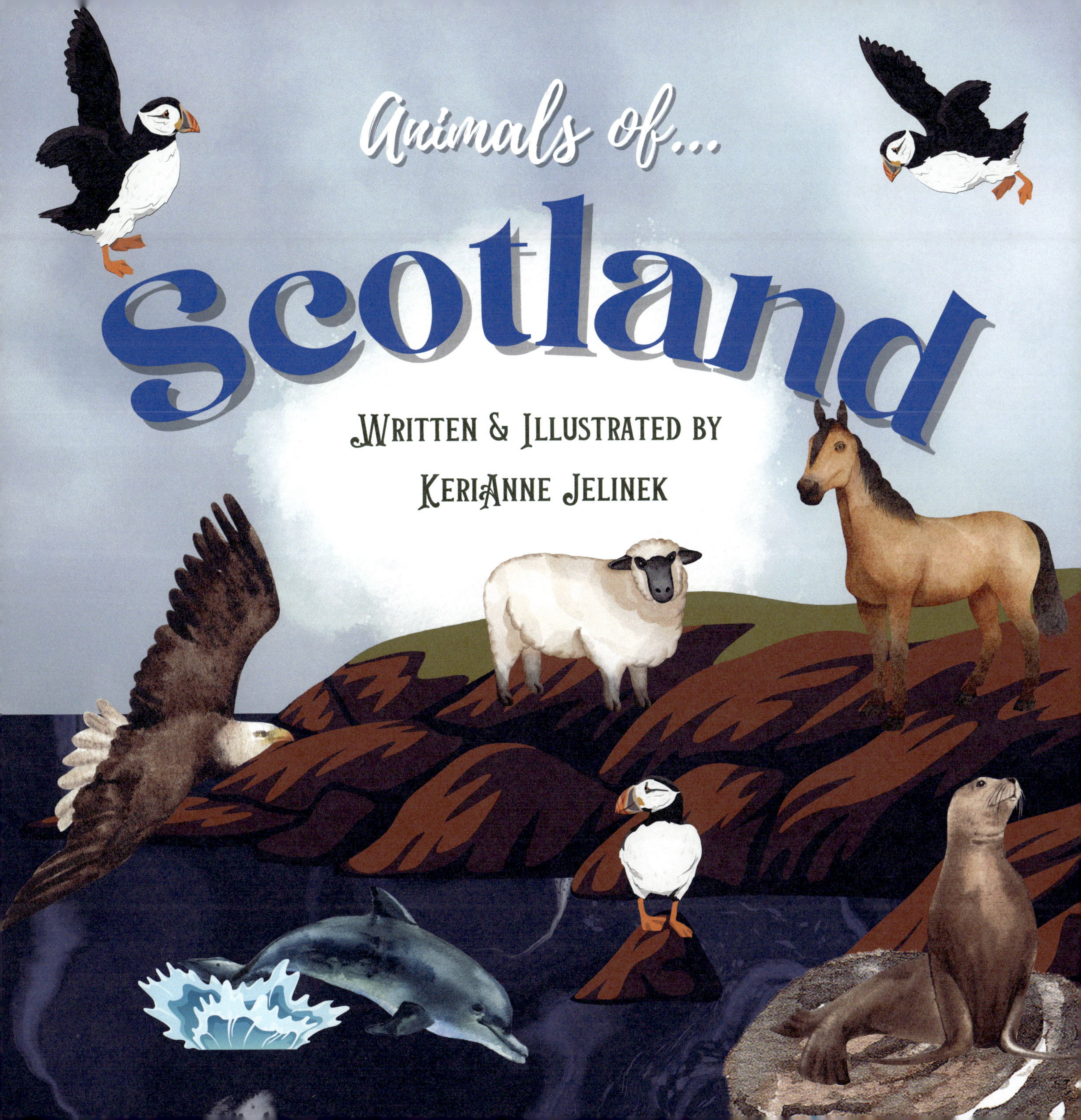
Animals of...
Scotland
Written & Illustrated by
KeriAnne Jelinek

I'm a rambunctious...
Red Squirrel

I'm a regal...

Red Deer

I'm an eager...
European Pine Marten

Scottish Wildcat

I'm a pretty...

Puffin

I'm a hairy...
Highland Cow

I'm an energetic...
European Otter

I'm a magnificent...
Mountain Hare

I'm a brilliant...
Bottlenose Dolphin

I'm a grand...
Grey Seal

I'm a magnificent...

Minke Whale

I'm a roosting...

Rock Ptarmigan

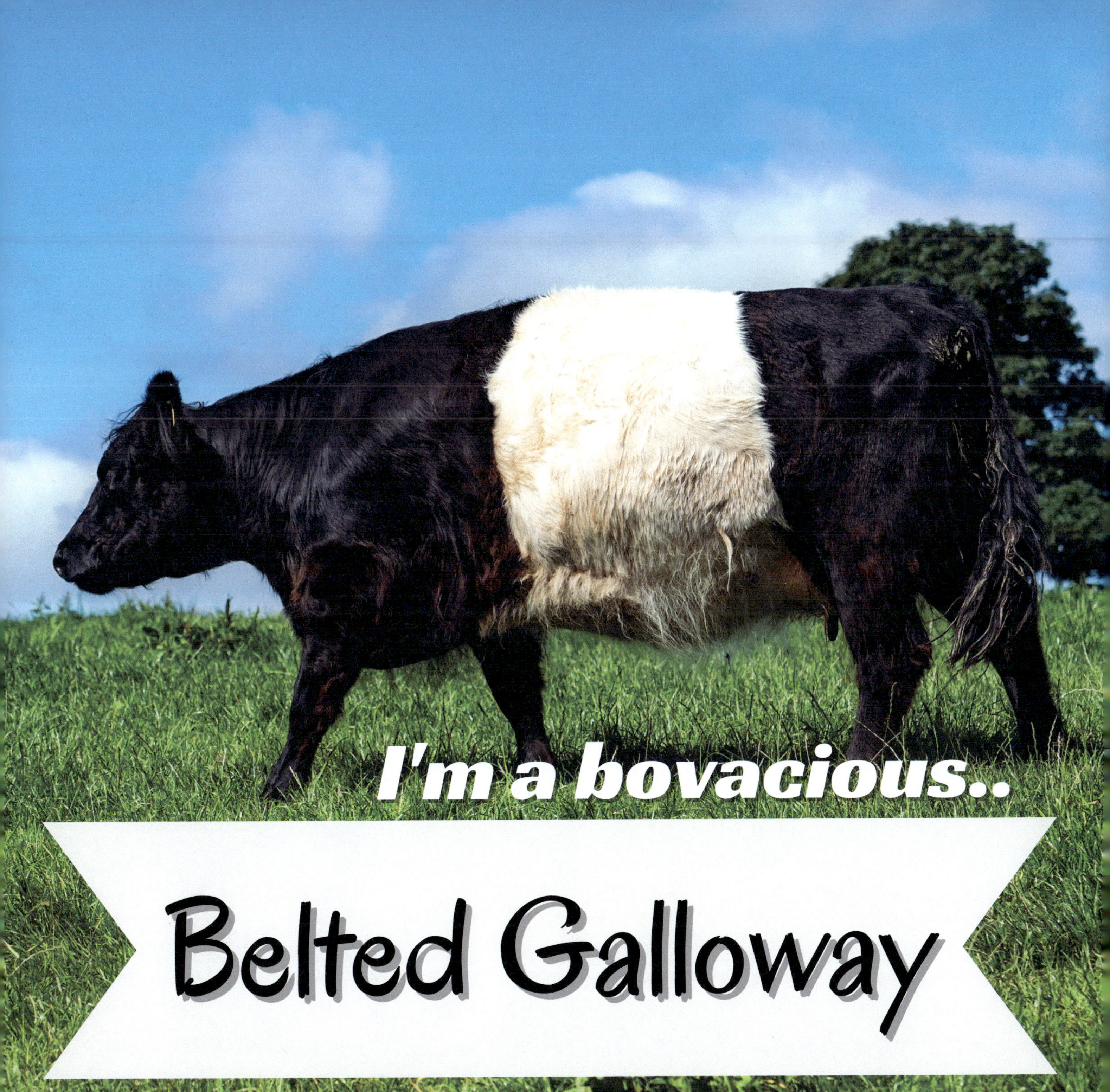
I'm a bovacious..
Belted Galloway

I'm a clever...
Clydesdale Horse

I'm a sleek...
Scottish Terrier

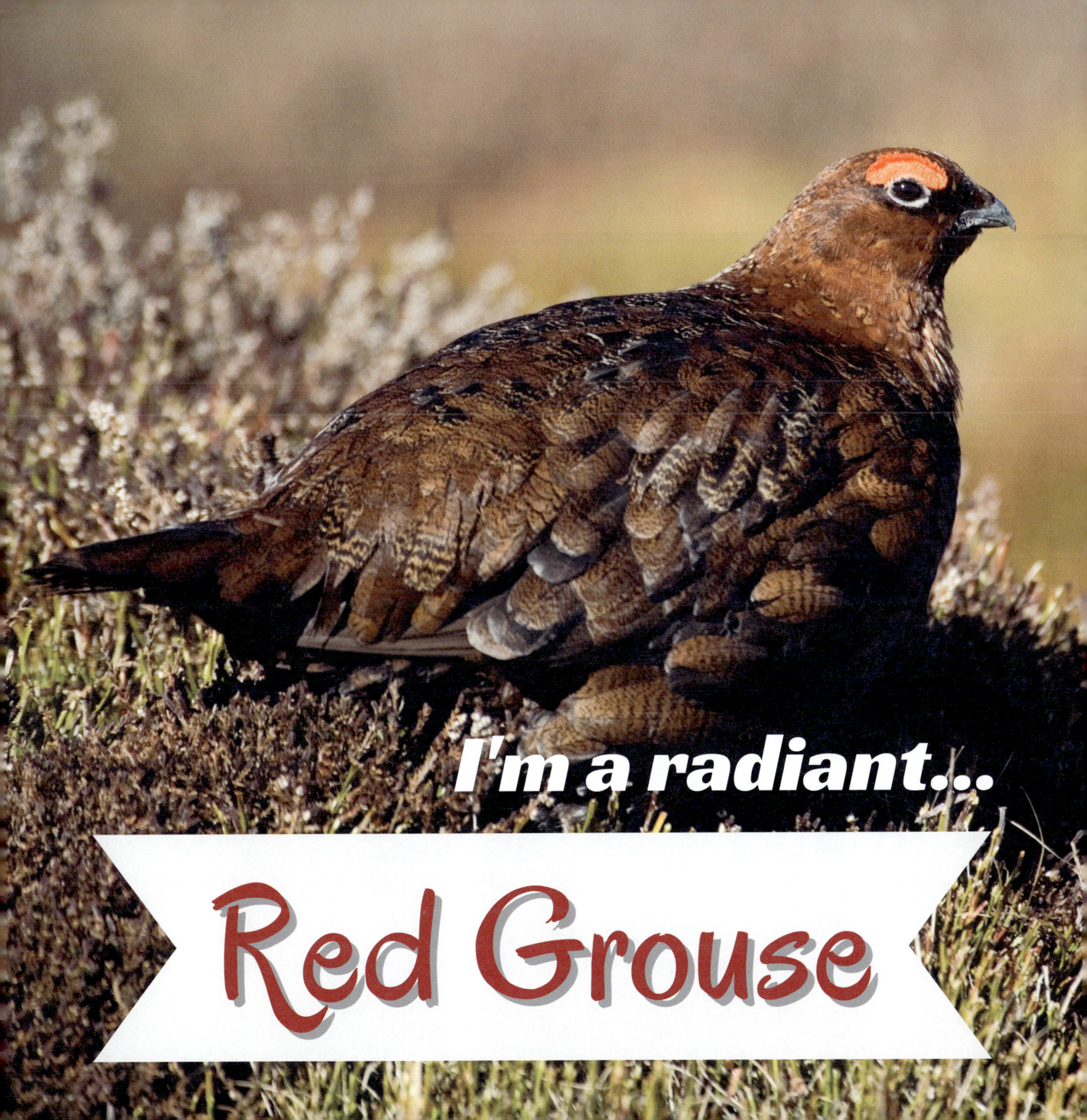
I'm a radiant...
Red Grouse

I'm an adorable...
Ayrshire Cow

I'm a handsome...
Highland Pony

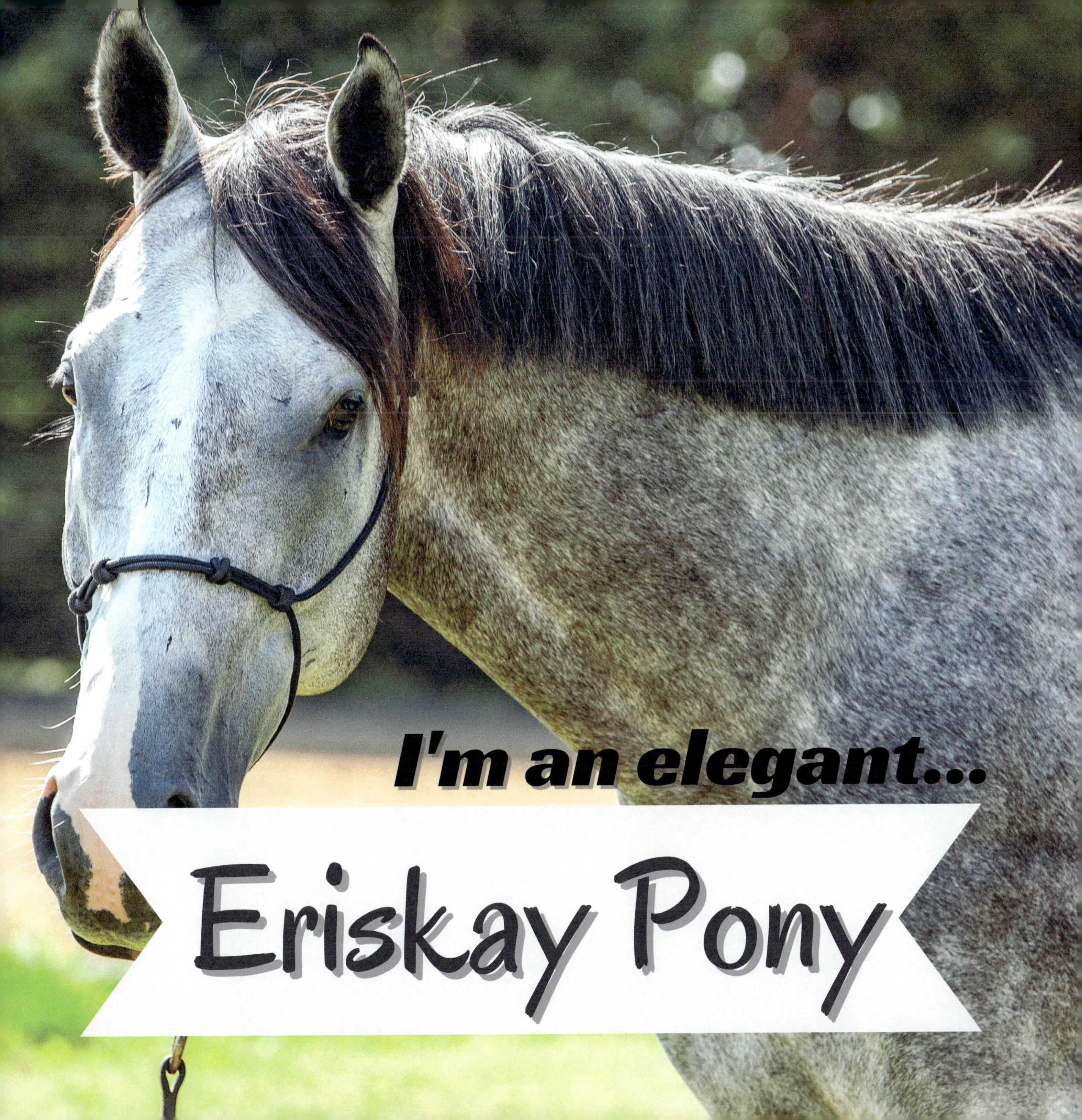
I'm an elegant...
Eriskay Pony

Scottish Deerhound

I'm a sheepish...
Shetland Sheep

I'm a cheeky...
Collie

I'm a wonderful...
White Tailed Eagle

Made in the USA
Columbia, SC
11 March 2025